In

My

Mother's

Kitchen

An
Introduction
to the
Healing
Power
of
Reminiscence

Second Edition

Robin A. Edgar

Tree House Enterprises

Charlotte, North Carolina

LIBRARY
~~WITHDRAWN~~ COMMUNITY COLLEGE
5900 S. SANTA FE DRIVE
LITTLETON, CO 80160-9002
303-797-5090

Published by
Tree House Enterprises
www.treehouseonline.net

© Copyright 2002, 2003 by Robin A. Edgar
All rights reserved. No part of this book may be reproduced in any
form or by any electronic or mechanical means, including information
storage and retrieval systems, without the written permission of the
publisher.

First edition 2002
Second edition 2003

Cover design by
David Adelman

Illustrations by
David Adelman
Jessi E. Adelman

Printed and bound in the United States of America

Library of Congress Cataloging-in-Publication Data

Edgar, Robin A.

In My Mother's Kitchen:
An Introduction to the Healing Power of Reminiscence
by Robin A. Edgar.-- 2nd ed. p. cm.

ISBN 0-9723770-7-7 (pbk. : alk. paper)

1. Reminiscing. 2. Healing--Psychological aspects. 3. Bereavement.

I. Title.
  BF378.R44E34 2003
  153.1'2--dc21

                                                        2003009191

To my parents, Jack and Sandra Babich, who gave me so many wonderful memories, teaching me to love to help people by their example.

NOV 15 2004

CONTENTS

Foreword

Twenty-six years ago, when my hair was still blonde and I still had a mother, there were only five books on grief.

> We didn't talk about it.
> We didn't write about it.
> We didn't do grief.

And as a result, we had more illnesses and more emotional struggles, and led more shallow, stiff lives. That has changed.

The Centering Corporation, which I founded with my husband, Dr. Marvin Johnson, in 1977, is North America's oldest and largest bereavement resource center. We carry over 500 books on grief and loss. *In My Mother's Kitchen* is one of my favorites.

My mother had a cheery kitchen filled with chicken figurines, chicken wallpaper and chicken curtains. Every time I walk past a gift shop featuring some strutting porcelain cock or beautiful sitting hen, I talk to Mother in my heart. I tell her how I'd buy that for her. And now on my kitchen table sit a neat couple — a hen and a rooster.

I wish when my mother died years ago I had cradled a book such as Robin's in my hands and done the exercises and smudged the pages with my tears and drops from good cups of flavored coffee. I invite you to do so now — and to remember your mother and other loved ones who never die because they are still alive in your heart and memories.

Joy Johnson
Co-founder, Centering Corporation

Preface

I lost my mother to cancer. Although I knew for a long time that she was dying, it was a challenge to cope with the loss of someone who was so close to me. At her memorial service, a friend told me how rituals of his faith, such as cutting the black ribbon and covering the mirrors, had helped him cope with his own mother's death.

Around that time, I was developing the syllabus for "Writing Your Life Story," a writing course for the John C. Campbell Folk School in Brasstown, North Carolina. Using written accounts of memories about my mother's life as examples for my students, I found great solace in recording our time together. Through these memoirs, I developed a personal set of rituals that helped more than anything else to ease the pain.

Eager to share my discovery with others, I began

teaching *The Healing Power of Reminiscence* workshop to hospice caregivers and volunteers. I discovered this concept was beneficial to everyone from children to seniors. In addition to helping people cope with the loss of a loved one, reminiscence writing can be an effective tool in coping with change due to illness or to separation due to divorce or empty-nest syndrome. Even genealogists and scrapbookers can use this step-by-step creative process for recording family histories.

The stories in this book not only identify and celebrate the wonderful qualities that made my mother who she was; they also define how her life affected me. Each reflection conjures up a meaningful lesson to be learned. I offer this book as an extension of my process of establishing rituals from those memories to help me cope with her death. More important, I present it as a workbook for others to develop rituals from the recollections of their loved ones.

As I teach *The Healing Power of Reminiscence* around the country, I encounter many individuals who are not initially comforted by their memories. Not all memories are about happy times. Some recount painful experiences or times without harmony. Celebrating the laughter and the lessons within is what brings comfort. It is my hope that *In My Mother's Kitchen* not only reveals the heart of a very special woman whom I cherish, but directs readers to a path where they can resolve this unhappiness and find comfort in their own grief.

The Promise

An Introduction to Celebrating Memories

Parents teach their children by example — even how to die.

– Martin Amis

When my mother found out that she had breast cancer, she did not tell me until she was home, recuperating from a radical mastectomy. "I didn't want to worry you," she explained, reasoning that my three children needed their mother and that I should not leave them to travel all the way from Ohio to Florida to see her. The next month, when school was out, we all flew down south for a visit.

While the kids were at the pool with Grandpa, my mother and I took a long walk around the big grass circle in her condo parking lot. Arm in arm, we walked and talked about life and what it would take to live with cancer instead of die from it. After endless rounds of tears and laughter, she stopped short and turned to me, finally able to express her greatest fear. Her steel blue eyes held mine as she spoke in her usual straight-from-the-hip manner. "I am really not afraid of dying," she said. "I am deathly afraid of being left alone in a hospital bed to die."

3

The promise spilled out of my mouth, straight from my heart. "I will not let you die that way," I vowed. "I will come to you from wherever I am to be there for you."

So, we made a pact. If she would agree to fight to live, I would agree to help her fight to die the way she wanted — with dignity, in her own bed. For her part, she waged a valiant battle, coping with chemotherapy and reconstructive surgery. Almost ten years after our agreement, when the cancer metastasized to her spine, she warred against it again, using radiation and physical therapy to walk again. It seemed that nothing could stop her incredible spirit to keep the promise.

She was up and around for about two years before she broke her hip and then, barely recovering again, fractured her pelvis. With my father's health in decline, my mother decided it was time to give up the fight. I watched that same indomitable will to live go to work in reverse. It was much harder for me to switch gears and help her fight to die.

On her last night, it was just the two of us in the condo. Before I closed her bedroom door, I lay my cheek on hers, so soft and warm, to say goodnight. When I checked on her early the next morning, she was lying there in the same position that I had left her sleeping in the night before. Only this time, when I lay my cheek on hers, it was cold, and I knew it was time to say goodbye.

Now and again, someone will remark what a wonderful daughter I was to keep that promise to my mother. I always smile and say: "It takes a wonderful mother to make a wonderful daughter."

How This Book Can Help You

This book is not just a testimony to my mother. It is also a workbook that directs you to use the sights and sounds of the past to celebrate life. Use each chapter like a stepping-stone, taking the time after each one to capture memories of your own.

At the end of each chapter, exercises lead you along a path to find and elaborate on specific memories. Your memory is like a muscle; the more you use it, the stronger it becomes. Sharing stories with relatives and friends about old family photos, recipes, sayings and jokes can be very good exercise.

Before there was a written language, societies used storytelling to explain and preserve their cultural history. Songs, chants, fables, rhymes and even dances preserved the memories of ancestors and explained the world that was both seen and unseen. Today's society still needs this powerful connection.

By the end of this book, you should have an adequate collection of stories that capture the essence of you and your loved ones. From them you will also be able to develop meaningful rituals if you need help to find peace for a personal, loss and to carry on your family's traditions.

1

Where to Begin

Follow Your Senses

There is no sincerer love than the love of food.

– George Bernard Shaw

The easiest way to discover the path to memory is to follow your nose. Odors such as bus fumes, chicken soup and the steam from an iron can open the floodgates of your memory.

Have you ever heard a favorite old song play on the radio? Isn't it amazing how you can not only remember most of the words, but also recall where you were and who you were with the first time you heard it? Photographs are another way to bring back memories as you recognize people, places and things from your past. Other objects such as old jewelry, baseball gloves or even dishes can trigger stories, thoughts and feelings.

The following stories are examples of how your senses can get you started on your journey.

In My Mother's Kitchen

My mother's kitchen may have been tiny, but as far as she was concerned, it was just the right size. She used to say, "I can clean the floor with two swipes of the mop." Every day at four o'clock, she would set aside her dressmaking chores and whip up the most delicious family meal, with barely enough room to turn around in that cozy space.

As a child, I would position myself in a chair by the doorway, my feet propped up on the white enamel gas stove to watch. As she chopped, measured and stirred, we passed the time, talking about everything from Grandma's bootleg wine that she made in the bathtub to what I wanted to be when I grew up. Whenever she lifted the lid of one of the pots, the aroma of homemade chicken soup or pot roast swirled to the ceiling, and the casement windows, wound tightly shut against the winter gray, would grow cloudy. It felt so warm and safe in my special place by the kitchen door. Sometimes, as an adult with children of my own, I wish I could still wedge myself between the kitchen chair and the stove and prop up my feet so we could talk — just once more.

My ritual: When I miss my mother, I cook her favorite recipes for my family and friends. As we sit around the table enjoying the meal, I feel warm and safe again.

The Friendship Ring

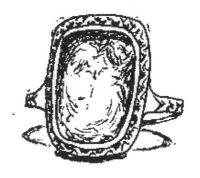

The top left-hand drawer of my mother's solid cherry dresser was a constant source of wonderment to me as a child; naturally, I took every opportunity to view its contents. I confess that my fascination often led me to sneak into her room when she was not home to look at and touch each item — like a pirate counting and recounting the contents of a treasure chest.

On the rare occasions when my mother dressed for an outing with my father to a fancy family affair, I would hold watch on the edge of her bed, waiting patiently for her to finally slide open the drawer and choose her jewelry. Sensing my curiosity, she would let my gaze linger over the shapes and colors. If there was time, she told me the stories behind the various baubles — the relatives they used to belong to or how she came to acquire them. With these tales, I wove a tapestry of fantasy and truth that became my family history.

One piece that was particularly fascinating was a ring of amethyst, my mother's birthstone. In its bezel setting surrounded by delicate golden filigree, the translucent purple gem looked to me like a sacred family heirloom. I will never forget the day she told me its true legacy. The story shaped my sense of who she was and who I should like to become as no other single event has in my life.

When my mother turned sixteen, she left high school and, as many girls in the early 1900s did, went to work. One of her co-workers, Toby, stood out from the endless rows of women who worked in the large office. Toby suffered from epilepsy.

The other women would not sit next to Toby at lunch and refused to help her when she had seizures, for fear they might catch her disease. My mother felt sorry for her, so she went to the library and looked up the affliction in medical journals, discovering that it was not contagious. When she brought the good news back to work, no one believed her. From that day on, Mom befriended Toby, sitting with her during lunch and helping her when she had seizures.

Eventually, her friend's condition worsened, forcing her to leave the job. On her last day, Toby took my mother to lunch and gave her the amethyst ring as a token of her gratitude for my mother's help.

I asked my mother why she kept the ring in her dresser drawer instead of on her finger. She explained that, because of her work, she only wore her wedding band on her left hand and did not wear any jewelry on her right hand. Then, to my delight, she promised that I could wear it when my ring finger grew bigger.

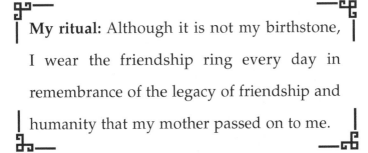

My ritual: Although it is not my birthstone, I wear the friendship ring every day in remembrance of the legacy of friendship and humanity that my mother passed on to me.

Breadbox Memories

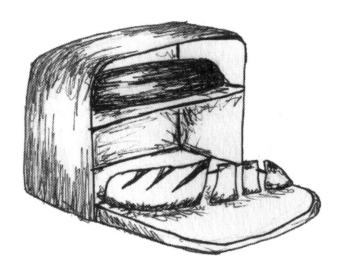

Jingling bells cut through the musty silence as we crossed the threshold of yet another antiques store. My husband's penchant to find the right handmade oar was taxing my patience, but I busied myself scanning the dusty bric-a-brac while he continued his search. My gaze fell on an object whose shape was so familiar that instinctively, I reached over and pulled the black plastic knob to open the door of a white enamel breadbox.

The creaking sound filled my thoughts with the contents of my mother's breadbox, which sat on top of the refrigerator in the corner of our tiny kitchen. The unmistakable aroma of her baked-from-scratch chocolate cake (without the icing because there was enough sugar in it already) came to me as if it were sitting there in its usual place on the top shelf.

On Saturday afternoons, my mother would haul out the old Mixmaster to make her wondrous cakes. I loved to watch as she deftly blended the ingredients, one by one into the mixing bowl. With a spatula in one hand, she would scrape the sides of the turning vessel while the other hand nudged the bowl to turn a little faster. Hypnotized by the motion of the creamy mixture swirling toward the center, I waited patiently for her to turn off the switch, eject the beaters and tap them on the side of the bowl before handing them to me to lick.

Almost able to taste that sweet, sticky batter again, I recalled another familiar item from our family breadbox. On the shelf beneath the cake, there was always room for the yellow and white waxed paper bag filled with the heels from pumpernickel or rye bread brought home from Richer's Bakery.

I started working at the bakery when I was 15. Although I was below the minimum hiring age, I lied and told them I was 16, which they probably knew wasn't true because they paid me under the table. After hearing my Aunt Jean's whispered conversations with the neighbors about how my parents would soon be out of money if my mother did not get out of the hospital soon, I decided the situation warranted this little white lie. Besides, there was an unusually long teacher's strike and I needed something to do.

When school started up again, I continued working at the bakery on weekends. On Sunday mornings, little old ladies barely able to see over the rounded glass countertop would hold up their numbers and watch me with their large watery eyes as I slid a bread down from the shelves above the slicing machines. Invariably, they would bark their common mantra: "Is it fresh?"

Although the fresh bread did not come out until yesterday's was sold, I was trained to always reply with a smile, "Of course it's fresh; that's all we sell." If I did not get a nod to proceed, I would obediently place the loaf on the counter so they could push and press the crust to determine the truth for themselves. Usually, whether it was truly fresh or not, they would shrug and smile, saying, "Slice it for me, dear, but not too thin."

When the early crowd finally cleared out and I had a little time before the afternoon group poured through the door, I would use the long-handled wooden brush to clean the slicing machines. I always tried to do this before one of the other girls came on their shift so that I could collect all of the stray heels of bread that did not make it into the customers' bags. I did this to bring home to my mother, who loved to dunk them in her morning coffee.

By this time, my mother had returned home from the hospital. As she lay in her bed, her blue eyes would brighten with her smile whenever I presented her with the yellow and white waxed paper bag containing the heels of pumpernickel and rye. Although she said she hated that I had to work in the bakery, she always thanked me profusely for remembering her special treat.

My ritual: I never did get the hang of baking scratch cakes like my mother, but I did learn to bake my own bread. As the fresh loaf comes steaming and luscious out of its pan, I can hardly wait to cut off the heel and eat it in remembrance of my mother and the smile it brought to her face.

Exercises for Chapter One

Round up some old photos or objects that will help you remember incidents and feelings from the past. Write down anything that comes to mind and tell someone about it. Before long, even a sentence or two can grow into a story as you share it with others.

If you cannot remember specifics about these questions, ask a relative or childhood friend to help. Often the details appear in the process of conversation. Write down your memories and collect some of the recipes. They do not have to be exact; just something to trigger similar sights, smells or sounds. Even if it's playing golf or eating a hamburger at your favorite place, you will be amazed how healing it is to remember your loved one this way.

What was your favorite dish as a child? Is there a special dish that you had at every holiday gathering? Do you have any family recipes handed down from generation to generation?

_____

_____

_____

_____

Did you have a special place you always went to when you dined out? Did your loved one have a favorite dish that he or she made or always ordered in a restaurant?

_____

_____

_____

_____

Are there certain aromas, such as those from cinnamon or sauerkraut that remind you of family gatherings? Do certain kitchen sounds — grating, chopping and the clanging of pots — trigger childhood memories?

_____

_____

_____

_____

Did your loved one always wear a special piece of jewelry or article of clothing?

_____

_____

_____

_____

Was there an item, such as a fishing pole or a set of golf clubs that meant a great deal to them?

_____

_____

_____

_____

2

Keep the Memories Alive

Laughter Is Good Medicine

A merry heart doeth good like a medicine: but a broken spirit drieth up the bones.

— Proverbs 17:22

Do you have any funny stories you love to tell about your childhood? Although certain things are not so funny when they occur — like getting caught playing hooky from school or running out of gas when you weren't supposed to be driving the car — laughing about difficult times after the fact helps you cope with frustrations you face in the present. Remembering with laughter can be very healing. After reading this chapter, think of the times you said to yourself, "This isn't funny now, but I bet I will be laughing about this years from now!"

The Birds, the Bees and My New Mascara

As much as I loved my mother, there were "times of the month" when I was a teenager when we really butted heads. When this happened, I would often spend the night at my best friend's, Lorraine. We would stay up all night and talk, mostly about boys, until we fell asleep. The next morning, the aroma of her mother's coffee would beckon us to the kitchen, where we sat around the table and talked the morning away over coffee and cinnamon toast.

Invariably, the conversation would turn again to boys. It was easier to talk to my friend's mom about this topic because there was an unspoken understanding between my mother and me not to go there. She simply did not want to know any details about her little girl's budding sexuality.

The first indication of this pact was when I started menstruating; I was almost thirteen years old. From the other side of the bathroom door, she slipped me a booklet about what was happening to my body. Other than instructions on how to pin the pad to the special belt, there was no further discussion — until I started to wear eye makeup on Saturday night outings. After several weeks of my experimenting with eyeliner and mascara, my mother cornered me in my room and asked, "Why do you wear all that makeup? You look like you've laid a hundred guys!" You can imagine the look on my face, let alone my friends', when I tell that story.

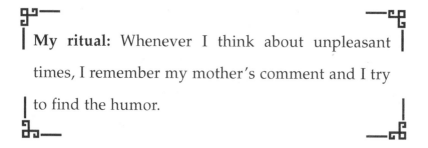

My ritual: Whenever I think about unpleasant times, I remember my mother's comment and I try to find the humor.

Reflections in a Hallway Mirror

As a child, I spent many hours gazing into the mirror that hung on the outside of the linen closet door in the hallway of our apartment. During the day, the door was swung open so my mother's customers could approve a freshly pinned hem or dart. But in the evening, as if to announce her workday was over when the last of her customers departed, she shut the mirrored door with a firm twist of the knob.

After my sister and I had gone to bed, my mother usually sat on the living room couch and watched television as she hand-stitched hems or beads into place. Our downstairs neighbor, Selma, often came over to keep her company. On the nights that I could not get to sleep right away, I would often skulk on my hands and knees along the hallway wall to spy on the grownups in the living room. Positioning myself so I could see the reflection of the television screen in the closet door mirror, I listened to the show. Better yet, during the commercials I could eavesdrop on their conversation, gleaning snippets of the latest gossip about the neighborhood that Selma always seemed to know in full detail.

I was particularly fond of my special post when my parents entertained. Frozen in position, I listened to their heated political discussions about candidates or world affairs until both of my legs fell asleep. The conversations, not meant for a child's ears, soared to aggravated tones, punctuated with modified expletives. Then they suddenly dipped to hushed rhythms that, to my dismay, escaped recognition. Giving up, I dragged myself back to bed where I fell asleep as I rubbed away the pins and needles.

I carried the secret of my late-night subterfuge into adulthood — or so I thought. One night when I was sitting up with my mother to keep her company while my father was out playing cards with his friends, she revealed to me that she knew all along. You can imagine my chagrin as it dawned on me that, just as I could see the television screen reflected in the mirror, so could she see me! We laughed about it as we sat side by side in her

Florida condo, but on the way home I wondered...what else did she know?

My ritual: Whenever I pass a tall hallway mirror today, it sometimes surprises me to see my adult face staring back at me. I laugh at myself and rejoice at how well my mother kept my childhood "secrets." Come to think of it, I am keeping a few of my children's secrets, too.

Company's Coming!

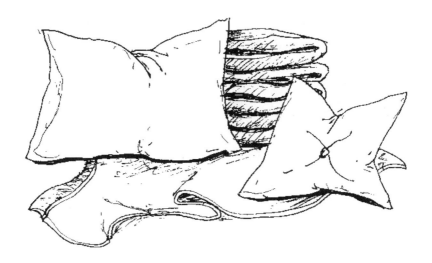

"**W**ho invited all these people?"

"What people?" I asked, pulling the cold plastic and chrome guest chair closer to the bed so I could hear mother's raspy whisper.

"And who is going to get up in the morning to cook them breakfast?" she demanded, raising her voice.

"Who are you talking about, Mom?" I managed to ask this in a deliberate low tone in an effort to lower her anxiety (even as my concern spiraled upward). I placed my hand, still cool from the night air, on her forehead. At least she wasn't feverish.

"The people that have been coming in all night long," she exclaimed, trying to pull herself up by the bars on her hospital bed.

My eyes finally adjusted to the darkness, and I quickly glanced at the other bed to see if it was occupied. Relieved not to see a sleeping form under the blankets, I turned back to my mother, her frail body barely discernible under her covers.

After palliative surgery to remove some of the cancer that had spread to her spine, she was unable to move, laying for weeks in her hospital bed like a pupa in a cocoon.

"You must mean the nurses who've been coming in and out to check on you," I offered cheerfully.

"I'm glad you're here to help put fresh sheets on the beds." She continued as if she had not heard a word I said.

I took a deep breath and tried to think of a different approach to the argument, almost choking on the antiseptic air. Staring into her steel blue eyes, I realized what I was up against. Those eyes, once able to soothe my childhood concerns, were simply unable to see past a post-surgery morphine fog. The small plastic bag hanging at her bedside slowly dripped the drug into my mother's vein, clouding both pain and reality. Convinced that she had awakened in her own bed to a house full of company who had arrived in the middle of the night, the ever-gracious hostess was fretting over the details of accommodating her guests.

If you knew my mother, you would know that her picture was in the dictionary next to the word "hospitality."

When someone came to visit, no matter how briefly, she always offered a cup of coffee or something cold to drink. Those were the rules. A stay of fifteen minutes or more also required food to be served. Although cheese and crackers would do, the old saying, "If I had known you were coming, I would have baked a cake," was her credo. I can still remember the box of candy in the hall linen closet that was forbidden to my sister and me because it was reserved for unexpected company.

"How about if I take care of it for you?" I asked, squeezing her hand as I tried my new tack. "Why don't you try to get some sleep and I'll see to everything."

"You should not have invited so many people at once," she chided, her tone softening to its familiar cadence.

"You're right," I said. "But now that I'm here, I can take care of it," I added, trying to apply the proper seriousness to my tone as I tucked the blanket under her chin. Sinking back into my chair, I waited until slumber finally softened her face. Secretly, I thanked God for waking me at three in the morning to come to her bedside. I let my lips linger on her silken cheek, relishing our moment together. "I love you," I whispered, and rose from my chair to turn to leave.

"You had better bring some extra pillows," she called out before I reached the door.

"Good idea," I said, holding back my laughter. "Good idea."

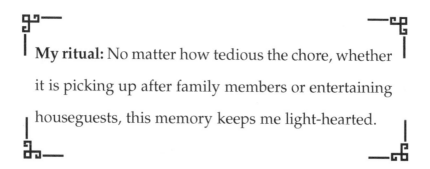

My ritual: No matter how tedious the chore, whether it is picking up after family members or entertaining houseguests, this memory keeps me light-hearted.

Exercises for Chapter Two

Although it takes courage to laugh at some memories, it can cleanse the soul. The following exercises will help you find the bright side of your memories.

Did your loved one tell the same joke or funny story over and over again? _____

_____

_____

_____

Was there an embarrassing moment you shared with your loved one, like the example of learning about the birds and the bees? _____

_____

_____

_____

Did your loved one have a special way of doing something that used to drive you crazy or secretly make you snicker? _____

_____

_____

_____

Was there a special saying or words of wisdom that your loved one repeated at every opportunity? "My great-grandmother always used to say..." or "If you ask me...." _____

_____

_____

_____

Did your loved one ever do or say something that surprised you because it seemed so out of character?

_____

_____

_____

_____

3

Look For the Lesson

Hindsight Is 20/20

Train up a child in the way they should go, and when they are
older, they will not stray far from it.

— Proverbs 22:6

Zig Ziglar, the famous motivational speaker, tells a story about the little girl who wanted to know why her mother always cut off the end of the ham before putting it in the oven. After quizzing each generation on why that was done, she finally asked her great-grandmother, who replied: "I did that so it would fit in the pan."

Part of who you are comes from things that happened to you as a child and how you were raised. It is amazing how the smallest incident can change your way of thinking, sometimes forever. As a child, I briefly became a vegetarian after seeing a live chicken at a petting zoo.

After you read this chapter, reflect upon why you do things a certain way, like the way you fold your towels or celebrate a holiday. Sometimes conjuring up memories that shaped your values can be painful because they are not always comfortable.

If that happens, turn the unpleasantness around by finding the lesson you learned from that incident.

Learning to Walk

*M*y cousin, Howard, says that being clumsy runs in the family. If that is true, then I hit the jackpot in the gene pool. As a child, my nickname was Flopsy, mostly due to my klutzy antics — like the time I ran headfirst into a bright red fire truck while on a walking tour with my fourth-grade class.

Although we lived up a flight of thirteen steps most of my life, I never seemed to be able to navigate the uneven terrain without tripping and falling down all or part of it. In fact, every morning as I left for school, my downstairs neighbor, Selma, would stand guard at the bottom step in her bathrobe, ready to catch me as I tumbled downward to my daily destination.

Part of my awkwardness was due to being severely pigeon-toed. When I didn't grow out of it, my mother took me to the doctor to see what could be done. He prescribed an awkward appliance called a cookie that, when placed in each shoe, could possibly straighten my feet over time. My mother did not want to embarrass me with having to wear the clunky shoes that went with this apparatus, so she decided to take matters into her own hands and train my feet herself.

That summer, we were staying in a large two-room apartment in the basement of a renovated mansion in Rockaway Beach renamed the Jefferson Hotel. It was there that she had me toe the line — literally. Every morning, after she braided my hair so tightly I had a perpetual smile, she had me follow the grid formed by the linoleum squares, keeping my toes turned out as I walked. She watched over me like a hawk as I put one foot in front of the other. Whenever my toes strayed off the line into the square, she would slap me on the back as a reminder to walk straight.

You may think my mom was too hard on me, but I don't feel that way. I will always be grateful for those walking lessons. I learned that I can overcome any bump in the road as long as I persevere and "walk the right way." And although I still have klutzy moments, I am often told that I walk like a fashion model.

My ritual: Whenever I feel defeated by a situation, I remember how my mother taught me to "toe the line" and I just keep going, putting one foot in front of the other.

A Pincushion of People Skills

My mother worked at home as a seamstress so she could be there for my sister and me when we came home from school. She learned her trade as a young woman when she worked as a pattern maker in the garment district in Manhattan. Then, shortly after she married, she had to open a bridal shop to support the family when my father lost the family delicatessen business.

When I came home from school, I loved to pull up a chair in the dining room where she worked. I would eat my snack, relaxing as I watched her fingers guide the fabric under the churning needle of the old Singer. The steady drone hummed the comforting message, "I am here. I am here." Raising my voice over the whirring machine, I would tell her about my day.

Sometimes I would come home when she had several customers waiting for their fittings. Always the performer, I would take advantage of my captive audience to read my poems or short stories, practice my piano lesson or show them my schoolwork.

During these times, I learned the rudiments of people skills as I watched my mother handle each customer. Some would try on dresses that were overly gaudy or too tight. If they were too vain to listen, she would keep her lips shut tightly around the ever-present mouthful of pins. For those who were friends or who would listen, she would pull out the pins and pronounce dictums like "That dress is not for you" or "I'd return it and get my money back, if I were you."

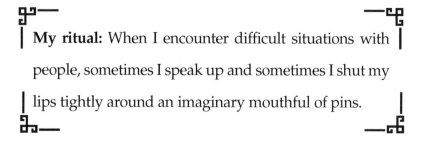

My ritual: When I encounter difficult situations with people, sometimes I speak up and sometimes I shut my lips tightly around an imaginary mouthful of pins.

Folding Laundry

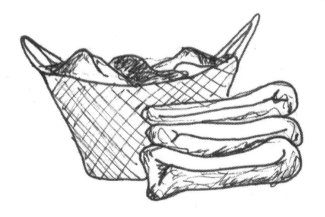

My mother spent most of her day in the dinette of our five-room apartment in Queens. A Singer sewing machine sat in the corner, always open for work unless we had company coming for dinner. The dining room table, where the family gathered for the evening meal, was covered with a special mat to protect the tabletop from getting scratched by the large, black handled scissors and pinking shears that she used to cut fabric. A radio, playing soft music, sat on one of the two corner cupboards that were bursting with boxes of seam binding, lace, buttons, threads, zippers and sequins.

It was in that room that I learned the art of mother-daughter conversation. I would wait patiently for my mother to look up so as not to distract her as she bent over her sewing machine, concentrating on a tricky maneuver. "What's up?" she would say as she pulled the fabric away from the needle and snipped the threads in one motion.

That was my cue to tell her about the ups and downs of my day. She listened as she trimmed a seam or pressed a dart, often passing on tips on how to handle situations that she had learned when she was a girl my age.

The tradition of conversation was particularly special on washday, when my mother took a break from her dressmaking chores to do the laundry. Although we had a washing machine in our tiny apartment kitchen, there was no room for a clothes dryer. Rather than lug a heavy basket down the flight of steps from our apartment to the steep concrete steps that led to the damp, dusty basement where coin-operated washers and dryers lined the walls, she would set up a large wooden drying rack in front of the window in her bedroom. She managed to fit a patchwork quilt of shirts, slips, pants and socks so they could dry there with the help of the radiator in the winter, and the breeze from the open window in the warm weather.

I loved to help her arrange each piece to the puzzle (perhaps that's why I'm so good at getting those last few items in the dishwasher today). My favorite part was when we folded the linens. Corner to corner, we matched the ends, moving together in our efficient little minuet. Like a family recipe, she taught me the secret to making the fitted sheets melt into a neatly folded rectangle the way the flat sheets did.

During these times, she shared the stories of her childhood and how her mother taught her to do the same things she was teaching me. Sometimes, as we folded, she talked about her own times of rebellion as a teenager — like the time she snuck into the bathroom in the middle of the night to use a chemical depilatory to remove the hair on her legs. The smell was so strong that it brought her parents and her siblings running to the door to see what was wrong. In between the stories of how to match the corners of the sheets, iron a shirt or clean the bathtub, I used these generational hand-me-downs to connect with my mother's childhood and construct the pages of my family heritage.

When I had three youngsters underfoot, oftentimes the most relaxing part of my day was when they were all bathed, pajama'd and tucked in bed. I would plop down on the sofa in front of the television and turn to the simple task of folding laundry. As my hands fell into a repetitive rhythm, my thoughts would fly away on autopilot. Whenever I got to the fitted sheets, the familiar motions would bring back memories of folding the family laundry with my mother and having those mother-daughter conversations.

My ritual: When my children were grown and called from college to find out what to use to clean the apartment bathtub (do not ask how long it had been), I was delighted to pass on the family "recipe." And, as an extension of my mother's mother's way, we took the time to catch up with wonderful conversation.

Exercises for Chapter Three

Someone once said, "You become what you look at." So much of who we are comes from what we observed our relatives, teachers and friends doing. On the other hand, if your memories are painful because the person involved was unfair or abusive, looking for the lesson that showed you how to act differently helps to turn that unpleasant incident around.

Use the following exercises to discover the things that influenced you to become who you are today.

Do you have certain rituals in the kitchen or the back-yard that come from watching your loved one?

_____

_____

_____

_____

Are your mealtimes regimented in a certain way, stemming from your childhood? Do you eat at a certain time, or always serve salad or dessert?

_____

_____

_____

_____

Do you say certain things in social situations or at work that are echoes of your past?

_____

_____

_____

_____

Who taught you how to do things like tie your shoes, hit a baseball or build a campfire?

_____

_____

_____

_____

Was there a time when someone taught you a life lesson by deed or example?

_____

_____

_____

_____

4

Treasure the Touchstones

Make Rituals from Memories

Rituals are repeated patterns of meaningful acts.

– Robert Fulghum

*O*nce you have mastered recording meaningful moments from your past, you can begin to find rituals to celebrate them. Practiced since ancient times, rituals are becoming more and more an integral part of the counseling and therapy profession.

They do not have to be intricate, time-consuming or costly. You can decorate a cube with favorite photos to keep on hand that help you remember. You can bake a favorite recipe or relive a favorite pastime. Simple acts like these should be easy to practice whenever the need to celebrate a lost loved one occurs. Practicing rituals is a wonderful way for generations to relate and connect with one another as they carry on family traditions.

The Mandel Bread Pan

My kids were all in bed and I was cleaning up the aftermath of macaroni and cheese and algebra homework. Something was stuck in the oven drawer and I could not get it to shut. After a one-sided wrestling match, I finally pulled the whole darn thing out, falling backwards and landing on my bottom. Accompanying this thud were the drums and cymbals of pots and pans crashing to the floor. From this new viewpoint I could finally see the culprit. That pesky mandel bread pan had managed to squirm its way out the back again and wedge itself between the drawer and the wall. It's not really a baking pan at all, but the bottom of an old aluminum ice-cube tray, the kind they don't seem to make anymore now that plastic is around.

My mother used this oddball utensil to bake her famous mandel bread, a semi-sweet Russian pastry that was my "If I were lost on a desert island and could have only one thing to eat" food. She discovered it was just the right size to bake my favorite treat in her toaster oven so she didn't have to turn on the big oven and heat up the whole kitchen.

Using a broom handle, I fished for this sacred vessel, dented and stained from years of service, and gently dusted it off. Carefully I placed it back in the drawer, so every year on my mother's birthday, I could pull it out and bake mandel bread in my toaster oven.

My ritual: For my daughter's wedding shower, in addition to her other gift, I gave her a set of old and dented aluminum ice cube trays that I had been saving for years. I included a card with her grandmother's mandel bread recipe, so she could carry on the tradition of love and good eating.

Birthday Dinner

*E*ach year on our birthdays, my mother would let my sister and me ask a few friends and cousins to come for a supper party. The best part was that we were allowed to pick out the menu. I always selected my favorite — meatballs and spaghetti.

This celebratory system worked well until I got older and did not want to have birthday parties anymore. Even for my sixteenth birthday, when my mother wanted to give me the kind of extravagant affair that my sister and cousins had had for this special occasion, I declined. I knew that my parents were struggling financially from the costs of my mother's illness the year before.

Determined to give me this rite of passage anyway, my mother contacted all of my friends on the sly, enlisting my best friend, Rain, to keep me out of the house while she decorated the cake, prepared the special meal, and hid my friends in my tiny bedroom. Rain arrived in the afternoon and suggested that we take a bus to a hangout where she had ostensibly arranged for us to meet up with some cute boys we had just met from Van Buren High School.

When the guys did not show, I was determined to stay out anyway and enjoy my birthday, in spite of the unseasonably chilly temperature for May. Try as she might, Rain could not get me to go home at the appointed time. Finally, an hour after we should have been home, she convinced me to go, saying we might have a phone message from the boys waiting for us. As we walked in the door, my friends came bursting out of my cramped bedroom, shouting birthday wishes punctuated with "It's about time!" and "What took you so long?" Then we laughed our way through a very soggy meatball and spaghetti dinner.

I never understood how much it meant to my mother to celebrate that special birthday until she found out she had cancer. Although her oldest granddaughter, Jessi, was only six years old at the time, my mother set a personal goal to live to see Jessi reach sweet sixteen. She kept that promise to herself, bouncing back year after year despite incredible odds. Toward the end, weakened and tired from her battle, she still managed to muster the strength to be around for that special birthday. Too ill to attend the party, she got to see us decorate the house and prepare for the festivities. A little over two months later, she allowed herself to peacefully fall asleep for the last time.

My ritual: Although my children now consider themselves too old to have birthday parties, I continue to keep the tradition of celebrating with special birthday dinners. Even though they have all left home and are not always with me to celebrate their birthdays, my children still get to pick out the menu for that special meal whenever we do get together.

Playing the Cloud Game

My mother was a very patient woman. She could sit for hours, stitching shiny little sequins back into their original pattern after letting out a seam on an evening gown. She also mastered the art of gently folding fluffy mounds of egg white into a sponge cake batter so that the finished product would rise to incredibly edible heights. Best of all was her ability to pass the time when we had to wait somewhere by playing the cloud game.

Faces, dinosaurs, horses and reclining figures formed before our very eyes at the will of the spoken word. "Look! There's a woman brushing her hair," my mother would exclaim, as she pointed to the tufts overhead. And, sure enough, if you stared and stared, the grooming lady would appear with unmistakable clarity before your eyes.

Playing with the clouds was our special game. Others could join in the fun, but nobody seemed to be able to spot the characters in the sky as swiftly as we could. It was as if our imaginations reached across the clouds and shook hands every time we played.

That's why I knew just where to take her the day my mother's strength had returned enough to go for a long drive. After lowering her into the front seat of my car, I loaded the wheelchair, her ever-present clunky metal companion, into the trunk of the car. We drove the short distance to the shore, where the two of us could view the wisps and swirls with unobstructed glee.

"Look! An old man walking with a cane," I cried as I nudged her chair into position to get a better view. "Like me," she chuckled, tapping her cane on the boardwalk beneath her wheels. "There's an elephant curling up his trunk," I added. We played this game back and forth until the sun settled into its bedtime sky, telling us it was time to go home. As we drove up to the house, she thanked me for sharing that sweet and simple game with her again.

My ritual: Now that my mother is gone, she is never very far away. As long as there are clouds in the sky, I look until I can find a figure among their wisps. If I am patient, she shows me one, and once again, our imaginations shake hands, and we are one.

Exercises for Chapter Four

Once you have found your memories, the rituals that follow will come. The following exercises will get you started on your journey. They are completely personal yet entirely universal. Have fun with them because they are yours to enjoy.

Make a scrapbook or a memory cube from old photographs. They can be random favorites, from a special
occasion or a chronology.

_____

_____

_____

_____

Practice something your loved one taught you, such as
a song on the piano or how to wear your hair a certain
way. _____

_____

_____

_____

Have a picnic at a special place where you both shared
good times or loved to go.

_____

_____

_____

_____

Name a pet or tree that you plant in honor of your
loved one. _____

_____

_____

_____

Tell a circle of friends the jokes or funny stories your
loved one used to tell.

_____

_____

_____

_____

Afterword

I have always loved stories. As a child, I savored the times after family get-togethers when the men would retire to the living room and the women would sit around the dining room table to discuss the age-old question: "What's new?" Rather than joining the other children as they ran off to play, I would pretend to be interested in gathering stray cake crumbs, nestled by my mother's side, as the women sipped their coffee and turned their tales.

My Aunt Claire was the best storyteller in the group. Able to turn a simple incident at the grocery store into a mysterious cliffhanger, she would punctuate one phrase with a carefully choreographed cock of an eyebrow or pause long enough as she twisted her charm bracelet for you to read between the lines. Although the particulars of those stories are long forgotten, the essence

105

of that connection still warms my soul.

Hopefully, the tools from this book will help you to find your own stories to tell. Whether you use them to pass on a part of the family history or to find ways to ease the pain of loss, I encourage you to continue to discover the amazing healing power of reminiscence.

EVERYONE HAS A STORY TO TELL

We would love to hear from you after you have recorded your memories. For information about how to send your favorite reminiscence to Robin Edgar, go to:

www.robinedgar.com

The Healing Power of Reminiscence

Acknowledgments

I am so grateful to all of my friends and family for the roles they played in encouraging me to continue with my work. To my students at the John C. Campbell Folk School, thank you for being my reminiscence test pilots. Blessings to friends like Diane Richard-Allerdyce, who knew what I knew about the healing power of reminiscence and worked shoulder to shoulder with me to reach individuals of all ages with our message, and to Sanna Morse, whose sense of humor and enthusiasm for my creative nature kept me going.

My sincere gratitude to Maria Teehan and Rita Stuck of Hospice of Palm Beach County, who arranged for me to teach reminiscence writing to their volunteers, and to Ruth Lindsey and Diane Park of Hospice of North

Central Ohio, for helping to make it possible to continue to hold bereavement workshops on reminiscence.

Kudos to Susan Tobias of HCI, who loved the first draft and pointed me on this journey, and to my editor Mim Harrison, who became my mentor, birthing coach and friend. Most of all, many thanks to my children, Jessi, David and Emily, and to my best friend, Gator.

Appendix

Hospice Contact Information

National Hospice and Palliative Care Organization
1700 Diagonal Road
Suite 625
Alexandria, VA 22314
703-243-5900
703-837-1233 fax
www.nhpco.org
info@nhpco.org

Grief Resources

Centering Corporation
Box 4600, Omaha NE 68104
402-553-1200
402-553-0507 fax
www.centering.org

For more information about scrapbook products or to attend a hands-on Home Class presentation, contact:

Creative Memories
1-800-341-5275
www.creativememories.com

Suggested Reading

Guides To Finding Rituals

The following books are helpful tools for establishing rituals for long-term bereavement benefits. The first book, by Laurie and Marc Brown, is wonderful for children.

Laurie Brown and Marc Brown, *When Dinosaurs Die: A Guide to Understanding Death* (Boston: Little Brown and Company, 1998).

Hope Edelman, *Motherless Daughters: The Legacy of Loss* (New York: Dell Publishing, 1994).

Robert Fulghum, *From Beginning To End: The Rituals of Our Lives* (New York: Villard, 1995).

Earl A. Grollman, *Living When a Loved One Has Died* (Boston: Beacon Press, 1987).

Marilyn W. Heavilin, *Roses in December* (Eugene, Ore.: Harvest House Publishers, 1987).

Harold S. Kushner, *When Bad Things Happen to Good People* (New York: Avon Books, 1981).

Doug Manning, *Don't Take My Grief Away* (San Francisco: Harper and Row, 1984).

Therese A. Rando, *How to Go On Living When Someone You Love Dies* (New York: Bantam Books, 1991).

Pat Schwiebert and Chuck DeKlyen, *Tear Soup* (Portland, Ore.: Grief Watch, 1999).

Gerald L. Sittser, *A Grace Disguised: How the Soul Grows Through Loss* (Grand Rapids, Mic.: Zondervan Publishing House, 1996).

Granger Westberg, *Good Grief: A Constructive Approach to the Problem of Loss* (Minneapolis: Augsburg Fortress, 1971).

Alan D. Wolfelt, *The Journey Through Grief: Reflections on Healing* (Fort Collins, Colo.: Companion Press, 1997).

Guides To Writing Family Memories

The following books are helpful tools in developing the writing skills to record your memories.

Bob Greene and D. G. Fulford, *To Our Children's Children: Preserving Family Histories for Generations to Come* (New York: Doubleday, 1993).

Denis Ledoux, *Turning Memories into Memoirs: A Handbook for Writing Lifestories* (Lisbon Falls, Maine: Soleil Press, 1993).

Bill Roorbach, *Writing Life Stories* (Cincinnati: Writer's Digest Books, 1998).

Bernard Selling, *In Your Own Voice: Using Life Stories to Develop Writing Skills* (Alameda, Calif.: Hunter House, 1994).

Linda Spence, *Legacy: A Step-by-Step Guide to Writing Personal History* (Athens, Ohio: Swallow Press/Ohio University Press, 1997).

Frank P. Thomas, *How To Write the Story of Your Life* (Cincinnati: Writer's Digest Books, 1984).

William Zinsser, ed., *Inventing the Truth: The Art and Craft of Memoir* (Boston: Houghton Mifflin, 1987).

About the Author

Robin A. Edgar conducts reminiscence-writing workshops in a variety of venues, including schools and art centers such as the prestigious John C. Campbell Folk School in Brasstown, North Carolina. She also facilitates workshops for organizations such as Hospice and The Alzheimer's Association as well as various scrapbook and genealogy groups.

Ms. Edgar helped to develop and run the Touissaint L'Ouverture High School Reminiscence Project pilot in Delray Beach, Florida. She also taught *The Healing Power of Reminiscence* workshop for the Hospice of Palm Beach County volunteer training program and as part of the bereavement program of Hospice of North Central Ohio.

The mother of three grown children, Ms. Edgar lives with her husband in Charlotte, North Carolina.

The Healing Power
of
Reminiscence

To contact Robin A. Edgar to conduct
a reminiscence workshop in your area
visit

www.robinedgar.com

Need Additional Copies?

For information on how to order *In My Mother's Kitchen*

visit

www.treehouseonline.net

BF378.R44 E34 2003
Edgar, Robin A.
  In my mother's kitchen